BE BRAVE

Saving Lives With Your Problems

ZACK QUILICI

Be Brave: Saving Lives With Your Problems

Zack Quilici

CKN Christian Publishing

An Imprint of Wolfpack Publishing

6032 Wheat Penny Avenue

Las Vegas, NV 89122

Paperback Edition

ISBN: 978-1-64119-117-3

DEDICATION

Justin Cutler on 11/08/2015. You led me through the prayer to surrender my life to Christ. A day I will forever remember.

INTRODUCTION

"Everyone has a desire to be real, but we just wait for someone else to do it first." — Alexis Feindel

There is a terrible emotional toll for people who go through something so devastating it is the foundation of their character. The foundation they fall back on when things get rough... the excuses they use when a situation gets uncomfortable.

When advice or a friendly presence doesn't work or doesn't register as someone actually being there for you, because all you've known is pain. The pain that stems from an experience that cuts so deeply the only result is that you are afraid of everything.

Your identity is in that pain. Who you are, can only be defined by the experience you went through. The secrets you keep inside. The person you see in the mirror, the insecurities that are developed- pain.

How is someone supposed to be brave if all they've ever known is pain and disappointment? What courage is there to rely on when your soul has been diminished through depression... anxiety, nervousness, anger, addiction, selfishness, heartbreak, divorce, abuse, abandonment, death, disease?

We learn that being honest is important. How important is it? Well, the honesty factor in any relationship might be the red blood cells. Transparency is so incredibly critical. The ability to speak up or ask for help. The courage it takes to talk about your experiences and the lessons you've learned.

How on earth are you going to help someone if you don't first help yourself?

Real freedom comes only from our Lord and Savior, Jesus Christ. He alone gives you the strength to be brave... brave about your problems, brave enough to withstand judgment from other people.

Scary as it may seem, be brave about your addictions, experiences or character flaws because you are a human being. Be brave and understand that whatever you went through or are currently going through- you are definitely not alone.

But, how is any type of healing going to happen if nobody knows it's happening? Imagine a marriage falling apart and the next step leads to divorce.

What if that couple knew of another couple who went through the same dilemmas, the same emotional roller-coaster that almost led them to divorce.

What if they could talk to that couple and ask for help? What if they were brave enough to admit that their marriage wasn't perfect?

There's amazing power in opening up, in understanding that we are all human and that marriage isn't easy.

It's not easy, however, to openly express everything that is going on in your life. The word *BRAVE* is a tough one. You probably think about a warrior who needs to be brave to slay the mighty dragon that will certainly turn his village into a French fry.

That's bravery, yes, but opening up about an experience or a character flaw is *Brave* as well.

Think about how devastating it would be to hear about someone that went through a depression and took their own life because they weren't brave enough to share their feelings.

That's awful, yes, but often people say, "I had no idea that was going on!" Now that, my friends, is my worst nightmare.

Maybe, if people could open up and share what's really ripping and tearing at their souls, they could give the courage to others to open up as well.

That's where real prayer and healing begins. I don't want to be haunted by the words "I had no idea."

Being brave is incredible. How cool would it be to save someone's life with your problems? What if YOU were the one that made that person smile and make them feel like they weren't alone with their problems?

What if you heard about someone going through something dark? Maybe you didn't necessarily go through it yourself, but you knew someone else who did.

Now, because the person you knew was brave about sharing their problems, their experiences are able to help the person you met who's in trouble.

What if this same person was in such a deep depression they're thinking about ending their life, but you opened up to them and admitted that you went through the same feelings, but made it out?

Your depression experience may just save that person's life.

Being brave is all about understanding what you are NOT defined by. You aren't defined by your problems, you aren't defined by your past. You aren't defined by your addictions, you aren't defined by your mistakes. You aren't defined by the things that hold you down. You aren't defined by your ego. You aren't defined by the identity that you are trying to uphold.

It' simple. You *are* defined by God, and your identity is through His grace. His opinion is the only opinion that matters.

Now it's up to you to be brave. This book is about my real stories and the lessons learned. The quote at the top of the first page, is about going first... this is me, going first.

I've decided to do what one of my favorite pastors, Carl Lentz said to do. *I'm using my pain as a platform and not a prison.*

This book isn't going to be a book full of advice for you. It's just me and my past problems and my stories- unfiltered. The *BEFORE* Christ stories.

Some stories have no dramatic ending, you might just have to ask me in person. The flow is off and so was my life. Heck, there might even be typos. The only thing you need to know is Jesus was my only answer. He gave me hope.

Now you can do two things with this book. *One,* develop your sense of bravery and live a Gospel-driven life. Become Christ's follower and allow him to gain your full trust. How is God going to change and take over your life if he can't have all your problems?

Two, bypass all the Christian stuff and just read the crazy stories and think, "Man I'd never do that," or "Oh, man, what a loser," and "Sheesh what a jerk."

CHAPTER 1

"It's in Christ that we find out who we are and what we are living for. Long before we first heard of Christ and got our hopes up, he had his eye on us, had designs on us for glorious living, part of the overall purpose he is working out in everything and everyone."
(Ephesians 1:11–12 MSG)

FLOORED

I press the accelerator and the engine roars to life. The speedometer reads twenty miles per hour. A song about the paralysis of pain blares from my headphones. I've been listening to it for days. With tears streaming down my face, I glance down again. Thirty miles per hour. Glowing beyond my headlights, white dotted lines marking the road blur into a single line. I normally loved the end-of-the-day drive home, but the word *love* confuses me now.

I floor it and pass forty. A familiar stop sign in my neighborhood approaches, but I have no intention of stopping.

Fifty.

Second by second, every lyric levels me.

Sixty.

I *am* paralyzed by pain, unable to stop what I'm doing.

Seventy.

Almost there. I don't want to slow down.

Eighty.

I scream at the top of my lungs. Everything blurs. I weep. I think, *I want to end this pain, shatter this soul.*

The check-in gate, attached to the check-in building, looms nearer. *Can it do the job?* That building suddenly becomes the answer to my pain. *It's easy, Zack. Just keep pressing down on that pedal. You're almost pain-free.*

Then, aloud, my voice cracks, "I'm done!!!"

❧

That night was a typical, bone-chilling November night in Reno. At least, I'd like to say it was a typical Wednesday night closing down the gym I worked at, but it wasn't. The chaos of the day was done, but deep down I was disappointed it was over. When the last person walked out those doors, I knew that my only company would be loneliness.

From blasting music, to motivating and inspiring people every hour of the day, my job was sometimes exhausting, but I was never alone. I had friends and conversations all day, which is a great way to pass the time when you're a people-person like me.

On my drive home, I usually slipped on my headphones to listen to relaxing music. Tropical rainstorms or alternative acoustic music were my go-to when I wanted to wind down. But in the days leading up to that eventful night, I'd been anything but relaxed.

"Paralyzed" by the singer/rapper NF had replaced my typical playlist. No matter how hard I tried to get away from selecting that song, I couldn't. My heart was broken.

I'd tap my cold finger on that track every time I got into my truck. The lyrics couldn't have been any closer to how I felt: paralyzed, and always cold, even when I wasn't outside.

I figured this guy had to have gone through something similar to write such an emotionally powerful song. In the span of his four-and-a-half-minute song, shame, guilt, and disappointment would wash over me every time.

That night, it'd only been three weeks since my devastating breakup and the bad news I'd received about my business—the one I'd worked so hard for, and that soon might be going under or in need of new ownership.

I didn't understand how I had gone from being the happiest, most confident person around to having sore eyelids from crying in between shifts. I didn't get why I had gone from having the dream girl, the dream job, and being the life of any party to being depressed, weak, losing weight, and just being flat-out sad and embarrassing.

Did I now fall into the category of "people who didn't realize what they had before it was all gone?" Was I suffering from idiotic complacency? I thought, *What did I do to deserve all of this torture?*

I exited the gym door, at least content with my work. Even if tears were falling, I still did my best to have the gym organized and ready to rock in the morning for my very dedicated morning coach. (Without her, I seriously don't know what I would've done. God bless her.)

Walking down the stairs, I always turned back after the first step to make sure the door to my "life" was secure. *Safe*, I said to no one as I continued down the stairs and to my truck.

And that's when things changed. My truck might as well have been a prison cell.

For the three weeks leading up to this night, the drive home was always the worst part of my day. That night was the worst of them all. Trapped inside, with my thoughts bouncing all around the cab, I turned the key and my truck roared to life. The winter air was lingering around thirty degrees with the wind chill, and the short trip from the gym to my truck had frozen me.

I hate the cold.

My evening commute was usually fifteen minutes and led me to the house I shared with my girlfriend and three other girls. *But*, I had to remind myself, *I don't live there anymore*.

Just a few weeks prior, my stuff had been politely packed up. (No sarcasm there: that *was* seriously nice of her.) But on that night, I didn't have a girlfriend *or* a house.

Thankfully, I had a place to stay at a good friend's house. Right when my life turned upside down, he had a room open up. That was a blessing, and I seriously owe him.

❧

So, I didn't take a right onto the freeway as I'd done for the last two years. It was more like a dreadful and seriously painful left—which might as well have been a left turn toward hell.

Because I now lived to the south in the beautiful gated community of Arrow Creek, my fifteen-minute drive was now forty. It had been home to me for quite some time—not home as a living situation, but as a getaway.

Previously, I'd spent thousands of hours at the community's country club golf course, not only as an employee but as a golfer. For two summers, I spent my days as a cart boy, sandwiched between morning and evening rounds of golf.

Now, it was eerie driving to a place that had once filled me with excitement. Each time I pulled through the gate, I was filled with despair. But, man did I learn how to swing a club.

Finally off the freeway, I had a long time to think about things, especially with that song on repeat. I entered a horribly long and lonely stretch of road that led to the community's security gate. I was drained. I felt sucked dry of tears, and I knew I hadn't been taking care of myself. I was a man on the brink—completely spent physically and emotionally. And on that night, I knew the road wasn't going to be very nice to me, because it wasn't the first time I had done this.

But that night was going to be different—very different.

At the four-way stop, no other car was in sight. Not that it mattered. I wasn't moving, but I sure was crying. I knew that a half-mile of straight road lay in front of me until the next stop sign. After that, it was about a quarter-mile to the check-in gate, which was a full-size house for employees manning the twenty-four-seven post.

I was ready to take some emotion out on this new truck of mine. If you knew anything about me, you'd know I'm the slowest and most relaxed driver ever. The word *fast* isn't in my vocabulary. But I'd gunned my V8 to full speed a couple of times before. It felt good, like I was releasing some negative, built-up energy.

However, when my foot slammed the pedal to the floor that night, everything felt different. My usual, happy ways had transformed into a dark and evil temperament. I questioned life itself at that moment. *Who am I? What does life even mean without love?*

So I floored it, and I didn't care what happened next.

Ninety.

I've lost my dream girl and my dream business. This is my nice-and-easy way out.

I closed my eyes and braced for impact. Then I heard . . . *silence?*

I closed my eyes for what seemed to be long enough to lose

focus on where I was driving. What seemed to be an eternity was only a few seconds. White knuckles gripped the steering wheel. My heart was racing. My breathing seemed to be uncontrollable.

I had pulled over on the right side of the road when I opened my eyes. A little crooked, but safe. *What happened?*

I knew what I had wanted to do. I knew that I wanted to end the pain, but it didn't happen. I wanted to end it right there. I wanted to meet my maker so badly I was going to purposely take my life. The only thing I remember though, was not remembering pulling over to the side of the road. Blackout.

Looking back, it had to have been God, right?

I was utterly messed up, driving my perfectly working truck to my perfectly fine living situation with an entirely flawless God ready to show his face.

That night, God got my attention. He had a purpose for me.

What I didn't know then was that God loved me and that he was aware of my intentions that night. He knew my state of mind, how fast I was going to drive, and that I was going to make it out of that situation. God saved my life before I knew it was God who'd saved it. He knew what he was doing.

And I think he had one word in his mind just for me during that cold night: son.

"See how great a love the Father has bestowed on us, that we would be called children of God; and such we are For this reason the world does not know us, because it did not know Him. Beloved, now we are children of God, and it has not appeared as yet what we will be We know that when He appears, we will be like Him, because we will see Him just as He is. And everyone who has this hope fixed on Him purifies himself, just as He is pure."
(1 John 3:1-3 NIV)

CHAPTER 2

You were taught, with regard to your former way of life, to put off your old self, which is being corrupted by its deceitful desires; to be made new in the attitude of your minds; and to put on the new self, created to be like God in true righteousness and holiness.

(Ephesians 4:22-24 NIV)

HITTING THE WAL

In college, Thirsty Thursdays at The Wal were my favorite.

After a long week of working and "studying" (what drink I'd have next), I knew exactly what was going to happen. I'd clock out from my part-time, penny-scraping job at Boulevard Pizza, a hole-in-the-wall, hidden gem of a pizza joint. I loved that place, mostly because I had cool bosses who were young like me and wanted to make work enjoyable. So, every now and then we said cheers together over shots in the house bar! At that time in my life, there was no better way to start a shift or keep morale high.

My first stop after getting off from work was right around the corner, to a little liquor store. I'd use most of my tips from that night and buy what, back then, might as well have been my God: good ol' Mr. Jack Daniel himself.

Man, what a great guy.

At the time.

I didn't know who he was or where he'd come from, but man did he make me happy! I clearly remember the many times I'd climb into my car to head home with my new bottle of happiness. Before I'd even turned the car on, I'd rip off the plastic, twist the lid, and smell the amazing aroma of Mr. Daniel's whiskey. I'd quickly put my mouth to the bottle and take a double shot of what I considered pure greatness.

On this one particular Thursday long ago, I indulged myself into the darkness the night would surely bring. Did I know it was wrong to drink and drive?

Of course I did, but my name was Zack Quilici, and I was way more attentive and athletic than everyone else. This night wouldn't be the last night my pride would lay me low.

And no, I didn't think buzzed driving was drunk driving.

While driving home to my fraternity house, I swigged down a few more shots, knowing that it was almost time to go to my fraternity's favorite bar: The Little Waldorf Saloon, aka "The Wal."

After what seemed like an eternity of lefts and rights, I finally made my way home without a scratch. (Oh, you thought I was going to have a drunk driving accident? I should have. God had yet to enter my life, but boy oh boy, am I grateful now that he protected me then.)

Walking up the stairs with half of the Jack Daniel's gone, I was "caught up" to everyone who'd been pre-gaming. (If you don't drink, "pre-gaming" means drinking before you go out to drink. No, it doesn't make sense.) Walking into my frat house, I knew it was going to be a fun night. The house was blasting with music. My frat brothers were shot-gunning beers and fist-bumping each other. They were frat guys being frat guys.

Cliché, I know.

I only had a few minutes to hop in the shower to get the smell of pizza and chicken wings off me. I knew that as much as drunk sorority girls love their pizza and wings, I didn't want them taking a bite out of me!

But I wasn't the only one in the shower. My friend Jack Daniel came in for the rinse-off as well. I took a few shots while showering, and then I took a few shots more while brushing my teeth. (You're not judging me for the alcohol drinking in the shower, right? But you *are* judging me for brushing my teeth in the shower. Tons of people do it! Time management was crucial on that night. Try it sometime. It could change your life.)

My beloved friend Jack was almost ready to say goodbye, and a few shots later, he was gone. Now I was ready to party like no one was watching. With the biggest, loudest speakers in the house, everyone knew when I was home because all they could hear was my music.

So, instead of trying to beat me with their speakers, they just came upstairs and joined my party. My room filled with my frat brothers and some girls who'd been invited over because, you know, if there aren't any girls around, it's not a real party. We waited for the bus, but it was not just any bus.

On Thirsty Thursdays, The Wal makes sure that every fraternity and sorority has an opportunity to visit them. So, they offer a free party bus. You only have to tip the driver a few bucks. All you have to worry about is getting home safely.

Yee haw! I heard the bus arrive. We shut down the party and ran to get inside the magical vehicle that was going to take us to the real party. Music blared as we kept chugging alcohol. (Of course, we weren't "allowed" to bring alcohol on the bus, but sneaking it on was pretty much a skill you had to learn if you wanted to be in a fraternity. I'm kidding, but we became pretty skilled professionals at hiding the goods.)

When we got to The Wal, I made sure to have my driver's license in hand so I could get in as soon as possible. I saw a huge line in front of The Wal, but there's a twist: if you arrive on the party bus, you get to use a different, shorter line. This made me happy because I didn't have to waste precious drinking and dancing time waiting in line!

The Wal had an awesome wood theme; like an old, western-style ranch house. It fit the description of the Wild, Wild West. With cool wooden logs everywhere, there was one you couldn't miss. If you're standing in line at The Wal, a huge, sanded, and glossed-over part of a tree separated the entrance from the parking lot.

It sat horizontally, was around thirty feet long and at least five-feet in diameter. This tree made it easy for the bouncer to keep the line nice and organized—as much as he could with a bunch of drunk college kids.

When we finally made it inside, I let out a "Woot! Woot!" I felt like Will Smith in *Wild, Wild West* walking into that place. Maybe it was the Jack Daniel's settling in that made me think I was some famous actor. During all the time and effort to get to the bar, I'd chugged a lot of whiskey. I felt that my night was already about over, and it wasn't going to be pretty.

❧

I scan the room for the obvious: a pretty girl I can bounce my pecs at and buy a drink. Then I see a buddy of mine I haven't seen in a while. Thrilled, drunken excitement takes over. I rush to say hello. He has a friend to his left, whom I don't know, and he's chatting with. I quickly get my friend's attention.

What seems to be an ordinary hug and a chest bump—another frat-guy thing—isn't turning out the way I planned. Apparently, I did something embarrassing as I hugged my friend.

I am so busy catching up with my friend that it isn't until the fifth time his friend tries to get my attention that I listen.

Cutting into our conversation, he yells over the music, "Bro! You fish-hooked me!"

I look at him, confused, "What?"

He quickly responds, "You put your fingers in my mouth!"

I laugh.

Obviously, I don't understand what is going on, but the sight of my laughter makes him very upset. He yells again and even pokes me in the chest to help me understand that I did something wrong.

Now I'm upset, yet still confused. And now he has touched me.

Back in the day, I did not appreciate being touched *at all*.

I say, "Whoa, man. Do we have a problem?!"

Yeah, I really said the most cliché movie line, ever.

He's quick to get things going. "Yeah, we do, man. You put your fingers in my mouth!"

I totally erase the fact that I have *no idea* what on earth he's talking about. All I'm focused on is that this guy touched me, yelled at me, and told me I did something wrong.

So, I throw a right hook to his jaw that put him out- cold.

He falls to the ground only to be stopped by his head bouncing off the jukebox.

Looking back, I can't believe that, over and over again, I decided that my ego was more important than someone's dear and special life. I put that man's life in jeopardy and I didn't even know him. Who was I?

But the party wasn't over yet.

I was instantly restrained by a bouncer from behind me, who locked my arms in place and shoved me toward the exit while yelling, "You got to go! You got to go!"

I was furious. I somehow managed enough strength to free myself from the bouncer, turned to him, shoved him and then—boom—I threw another right hook squarely into the bouncer's face.

If you know anything about how bar fights work, attacked bouncers have free reign to attack back. They can get you out of their bar any way they please. So, I was on the road to a lot of hurt.

By this point, I was outside of the bar, and was tackled.

And remember that big ol' tree? That guy was about to be my best friend.

As the punches flew, I curled up into a ball to protect myself. Not all the bouncers were wailing on me, but the bouncer I'd punched was getting his revenge and the others were just making it a little easier for him to do so.

They definitely got me good.

Blood was everywhere, but I was still conscious and my ego was still intact. *If I don't get knocked out, they're weaklings*, I thought. I was still tucked into the corner of the entrance of the bar and the big tree. Then I went flying.

Their teamwork was fantastic. They picked me up and tossed me like a bag of dog food up and over the five-foot-high tree. But when I landed, I thought they could've done better.

I didn't entirely clear the tree on my way to the parking lot floor. Rather, I landed *on* the tree, which had plenty of sanded-off branch nubs sticking out. I remember having bruises everywhere from those suckers.

Twisting and turning to the ground, I was lucky that my head wasn't the first thing to hit the ground.

Ha! Still didn't get knocked out! Pansies!

But I couldn't say that out loud because my lip was busted wide open and the taste of blood wasn't pleasant, especially compared to the God-sent taste of whiskey.

As I walked about a mile back to my frat house, still drunk and bleeding, I wasn't regretful. I was proud because I didn't lose. I considered my earlier knockout made up for the butt-whooping I received later. I called that a tie!

I barely made it a quarter of the way back before I decided to sit on the stairs of the basketball arena entrance and call for help.

I tried my dad first, even though we hadn't talked in quite some time. Why him first? No idea. Did he pick up? Nope. I left a voicemail I quickly forgot. Then I hung up and called my loving and always-answering mother.

Before I was even into the details of why I needed a ride, she was already on her way. I guess I was just going to leave the reasons for her arrival.

I think it was around midnight when all this happened. Forgive my memory. I now believe I'm still suffering from the concussion I got that night.

When my mom picked me up, saw me, and heard my

story, she was equally worried and disbelieving. There may have been some words of motherly advice and verbal smacks to the face. But who knows? I was hammered.

She took me to the hospital, where they conducted a CT scan of my noggin. It was negative for fractures, but it was obvious I had a concussion.

I had a black eye, a gash in my lip (that just wouldn't stop bleeding), and bruises everywhere from that giant tree, but I was alive.

Not bad, I thought, *but man was I lucky.* Or so I thought.

Looking back, luck had nothing to do with it. Neither did my ego. Being called the "One Hit Wonder," (a nickname I'd been presented with from the witnesses of my many knockouts), wasn't cool.

Was I proud that I was a "manly man" who only needed one punch to knock someone out? Who was I kidding? Nothing is cool or manly about any of that.

But despite that night, I was okay, and I've learned that it's cooler to be nice. After that night, I planned on making sure that kind of night never happened again.

What I didn't know is that there was already a plan, and it wasn't mine.

It was God's.

The LORD Almighty has a day in store
for all the proud and lofty,
for all that is exalted
(and they will be humbled)
(Isaiah 2:12 NIV)

CHAPTER 3

Refrain from anger and turn from wrath; do not fret—it leads only to evil.
For those who are evil will be destroyed,
but those who hope in the LORD will inherit the land.
(Psalm 37:8-9 NIV)

VIOLENCE HURTS

I can't believe 150 of my Facebook friends have confirmed they're coming to my twenty-first birthday party tonight. Then again, maybe I can. I've only been thinking about it and planning it for the last three months. Everyone and their mom got an invitation. I made sure that every detail in the event was in order and that if anybody had any questions, I decided to even put my personal cell phone number down to make sure everyone got what they wanted. Friends inviting friends, excitement beginning to brew. Let's rage.

Cops were always the issue with house parties. They were such party poopers that made me sick to my stomach every time they would break one up, or was that the alcohol? I would definitely experience a big shot of adrenaline every time a party that I was at got busted. From jumping fences, to sprinting down streets, to keeping quiet, shutting off the lights and acting like they didn't know we were inside, we did all sorts of things just in order to get away with some partying. All those tricks usually worked, but a couple times they didn't. I got caught and cited as an underage drinker twice! That wasn't cool, nor was it cheap.

I definitely didn't want *this* party to get busted, so I did some research... apparently you can get a permit for a house party.

Yep, you can get an event permit for, duh, an event. I looked online and most of the time these permits were issued for weddings. It seemed that you had to go through the city hall to get the paperwork for such an event. But I got it done.

With the permit, music, beer, tons of drinking games, a stripper pole and a designated dance floor, the house was ready to rock-n-roll! This night was definitely going to be one to remember. I couldn't wait for the sun to go down. I was wired. I wanted this party to be a hit more than I wanted gifts. 10 out of 10 times I'd want my friends to come together and have a blast rather it making it about me.

The music was vibrating the entire block, neighbors were probably losing their minds already. Or were they? We actually had to alert the neighbors and hand them a written warning about the festivities to attain the permit. It was also an invitation most of the neighbors took advantage of, which was rad! I totally remember the next door neighbors asking for refills over the fence!

The cops decided to show up.... I was super surprised. I got angry and sad at the same time. Answering the door, I was asked "Are you Zack?"

I politely answered, "Yes, I am, what can I do for you guys?"

The officers were very nice, they understood and mentioned that they knew of the permit. They just simply asked me to do two things. "One, turn it down a bit; two, we are going to be here all night, waiting for drunk drivers to pull away from your party, so I'd suggest if you want to keep some friends safe, a little announcement is highly recommended."

Phew! Right when I closed the door on the cops, I got an invite that was going to change my life forever. One of my best friends invited me upstairs to my room. I walked through the door, which he quickly closed, as if he was trying to hide something. He was. He had made a huge line of cocaine just for me.

Up until that point in my life, I had never done cocaine. I only knew that it was one of the craziest drugs out there.

He looked at me, and I looked at him. I gazed at the line of cocaine that was sitting on my night stand with a glow from the light and said, "Why not?"

It might as well have been the devil in disguise that said, "Zack, you only turn 21 once."

With all the scenarios in the world going through my head at that very moment, staring at that neat line of powder, I probably didn't blink for two minutes. My friend broke the silence.

"I have another gift for you." It was a 100-dollar bill, and he quickly laid it on the nightstand and started to roll it up.

So, of course I did it. It was harder than I thought it was going to be- having to inhale hard and plugging one side of your nose and having the dexterity to get it all in one attempt was not something I was used to.

Did I feel good or what? It was like a shot of adrenaline, but a controllable one. Walking back downstairs I was a new man. The music hit my chest more than ever. In fact, it didn't hit my chest at all, it hit my soul. Cocaine was my new best friend.

I played a couple games of beer pong, roamed around, hit the dance floor and had tons and tons of conversations. Around 3am, things were dying down. I was totally bummed out, especially being drunk and crazed on cocaine. I wasn't even close to being tired. This party was the coolest party I'd ever attended, much less planned, so of course, I wanted it go on.

The process to shut down a party of this size is not an easy one. There were still around a hundred people at my house and it was close to three in the morning! There were multiple nice announcements made by my mother, but to most who hadn't met or didn't know her, she was just this old lady telling them they had to leave.

Some politely understood and left, and some said okay, but rolled their eyes after my mom moved on to the next group. This made my mom very impatient, and she even went to the garage, turned on the lights and opened the garage door- a perfect signal of closure of the party.

So... unintentionally, the party moved to the street. Everyone was hanging out and waiting to see what the next step of their night might be. More people were pulling up to attend the party, and one group was walking towards the house, when they should've been leaving. When they got close enough, my mother told them that the party was over. But, there were still a lot of people at the house and the music was still blasting.

"The party is over!" my mother said. She was pretty agitated by this whole, "The party's over" ordeal. One of the girls in the group walked right past my mom, but Mom quickly rerouted herself right in front of the girl and again exclaimed, "I said, the party's over!"

The girl was furious and obviously intoxicated. She screamed, "Who are you?"

My mom was drunk, she was tired, and she wanted this to be over. "I'm the owner of this house, and I'm telling you, the party is over!"

The girl AGAIN took a few steps past my mom. Mom quickly grabbed her arm and hollered, "Leave right now, the party is over!"

The girl quickly ripped her arm away and smacked my mother right in the face!

It happened so quickly, and up to that moment, all I had been doing was watching. But when the slap happened, I was *unfortunately* not just watching anymore. I say *unfortunately* now, because what I was about to do was breathtaking.

I lost control. Someone had just slapped my mom right in the face! I couldn't breathe or see straight; the effects of the cocaine and alcohol were leaving, but Mr. Adrenaline was making an appearance, once again.

I ran over, grabbed the girl by her throat with both of my hands, used all my power and squeezed. Then I lifted her off the ground by the throat and slammed her as hard as I could onto the asphalt of the street in front of the house.

Breathing heavily, I then saw that she was lying still and not breathing at all. She was lifeless on the ground. Did I kill her? I had just overpowered and abused a woman. How did that happen? What was wrong with me? Did I really just do that?

Wake up. Please wake up!

Protecting my mother, at all costs, was the only thing I remember thinking about during that altercation. Protection. Did that make it okay to physically abuse another human being? Let alone a girl?

I had always been taught and knew that it was never

okay to abuse a woman, REGARDLESS of the situation. I was now sick to my stomach knowing that the poor girl probably didn't mean to slap my mom. If it wasn't for alcohol, this would've never happened. It was 3am; everyone was drunk, everyone overreacted.

WAKE UP!

God was on my side that night, The girl was only unconscious for about 10 seconds before she woke up. She didn't seem hurt at all; she was just confused about what had happened, and she started balling her eyes out, saying, "Sorry for what just happened, okay? I'm so sorry!"

Why was *she* saying sorry... yeah, she slapped my mom, but that didn't deserve being body-slammed to the verge of death!

I felt horrible... I felt like less of a man, in fact. I wasn't a man at all. I was a coward! A coward that put my mom in that situation with this stupid party.

I stammered, "Don't apologize... I almost killed you! I'm so, so, so sorry! My goodness, what can I do?"

Emotions were crazy at this point, but she wanted nothing more than to just leave and forget it ever happened. Stunned, shocked, nauseated, high, drunk, regretful. What had I just added to my resume of sins? Abuse, battery, assault, whatever you wanted to call it, it hurt my soul tremendously.

My poor mother! Her face, her heart, all the tears, the beautiful back yard of this wonderful house that she had worked so hard on to make pretty, was completely ruined. The grass was smashed. It might as well have been called mud at this point.

She didn't say she was upset, but I knew my mom, and she was crushed inside. It wasn't the yard so much as the fact that her son had almost destroyed a girl in his rage that hit her right in her heart.

When it comes to protecting my mom in this certain situation, does it make it okay to violently attack a female? I thought so at that moment. Whoever and whatever attacked the person who gave birth to me deserved to have some retaliation coming their way. Regardless of what happened or why my mom got attacked, family is family.

For most men, that would usually be the right decision, being the protector of the family. Every man knows that their role of being a manly man is inherited as a birthright. They are expected to be the rock of the family and never show emotion. When the family is under distress, most family members turn to the man for a way out, a sign of relief, some muscle to barricade them with safety.

However, putting a man on a pedestal as a stress reliever does not take into account that men are only human with their weaknesses and faults. Men shouldn't have to be the only rock of the family! Jesus is the rock.

Don't act out of aggression because you think that's the manly thing to do, or because you want to be known as the guy who will stand up for his family for anything.

Don't get me wrong, standing up for your loved ones is NEVER a bad thing, but if there is a way out of the situation other than violence, take it, and don't be scared of what's going to be "thought" of you.

Besides, being all hulked out in a rage is never a good look; the faces you make and the spit you spew while you are yelling at another person are *sooo ugly*. Imagine what kind of faces you make when you actually start being violent. It's disastrous!

I think a boomerang is a perfect metaphor... if you are violent to another human, it will come back at you, every time! Maybe not in violence being inflicted upon you, but the feelings of guilt burden your soul more than a broken nose ever could.

The guilt I'm faced with can only be overcome with God's grace. The willingness to understand that I made a huge mistake hurting that girl, it's a real-life burden. I understand that I had a choice to learn from it, and I did. Would I do things different nowadays? My goodness, yes!

First, I'd probably not be overwhelmingly drunk at 3am, and second I would NOT live by the "eye for an eye" rule. That doesn't get anyone, anywhere.

When my mom was physically attacked, I could've deescalated that situation in many different ways, but didn't. Now, the best news I can share with you is the gospel of Jesus Christ.

The gospel has taught me that it's not okay to get drunk and lose yourself. That whole episode wouldn't have happened if I hadn't idolized the idea of celebrating my 21st birthday by throwing a huge drunk-fest.

So, the lesson? Don't attack another human. Be strong by being okay with the idea of looking weak. Turning the other cheek is far better than hitting someone else in the cheek. Not cool man, not cool.

Do not envy the violent or choose any of their ways.
(Proverbs 3:31 NIV)

CHAPTER 4

Brothers and sisters, I do not consider myself yet to have taken hold of it. But one thing I do: Forgetting what is behind and straining toward what is ahead, I press on toward the goal to win the prize for which God has called me heavenward in Christ Jesus. (Philippians 3:13-15 NIV)

COWARD

Waking up sore, everywhere. Was it from the previous day's work-out during our football spring conditioning program or was it from the twelve shots of Jack Daniel's I drank at the bar last night?

How did I get home? Stumbling outside, I see that my car is there, parked perfectly. I drove home drunk, like usual, because I knew how athletic and awesome I was. So getting in an accident, drunk or not, was not in my future. (*Wow...*)

Stumbling back inside, I bumped into the side of the door, knowing I screwed up, again. "I'm such an idiot," I muttered.

I stumbled to the sink to get some water. Leaning over to drink straight from the faucet, and almost throwing up after chugging a gallon of water, I decided to lie back down. I knew what was planned for later that day. I knew what kind of opportunity was out there, starting in a couple hours, on the football field at the University of Nevada, Reno. It was Pro Day.

Fifteen NFL teams were attending to watch the top players at Nevada go through combine-like drills to see if the players had what it took to make it to the big leagues.

I wasn't a starter at Nevada, but I had skills. It's just that I never cared enough to put the work in. I got *tons* of affirmation that I was good enough from my fellow teammates, but again, my attitude about life's opportunities just wasn't there.

Ha... What's that saying? "Talent without a work ethic..." Look what it does to your brain.

I was a wide receiver with great hands and great route running. I was 6'1 and 205 pounds. I maintained a 4.49 forty-yard dash, and a 34-inch vertical jump. I could bench press 225 pounds 15 times; my broad jump was 10 feet, 1 inch. But honestly, those never got a chance.

I was recruited by a tight-end coach, which was a completely different position. He obviously wasn't going to be the dude that I was going to deal with every day. The guy that *was* my coach didn't recruit me.

To my mind, that meant he didn't care about me. So, not only did I not use my talents, I also used my coach's rejection as an excuse to be incredibly lazy and drink tons of beer.

Long story short, I didn't show up for Pro Day. Don't ask me why, because I don't know. It's been a long time since that day when my future dreams ultimately ended. I can't remember my last day or when I decided not to show up.

Thinking about it now makes me feel nauseated. I was being a coward, that's the only thing that comes to my mind. I was afraid of hard work. Remembering how I acted hurts my heart, and it hurts bad.

All I know now is that it was all God's work. I don't think I'd ever have met him, if it wasn't for my lousy decisions up to the point of my salvation.

❧

This is a short chapter, because honestly, I'm sick of writing it. I don't like it, but felt the need to put it in this book. Just do what Colossians 3:23 says to do: *Servants, do what you're told by your earthly masters. And don't just do the minimum that will get you by. Do your best. Work from the heart for your real Master, for God, confident that you'll get paid in full when you come into your inheritance. Keep in mind always that the ultimate Master you're serving is Christ. The sullen servant who does shoddy work will be held responsible. Being a follower of Jesus doesn't cover up bad work. (Colossians 3:23 MSG)*

Every good and perfect gift is from above, coming down from the Father of the heavenly lights, who does not change like shifting shadows.
(James 1:17 NIV)

CHAPTER 5

Do not love the world or anything in the world. If anyone loves the world, love for the Father is not in them. For everything in the world—the lust of the flesh, the lust of the eyes, and the pride of life—comes not from the Father but from the world. The world and its desires pass away, but whoever does the will of God lives forever.
(1 John 2:15-16 NIV)

ADDICTED

I'm in my truck and I'm really fast.

Who cares? No one's around to see it, or hear it, for that matter.

Usually, the urge is too powerful to overcome. If something isn't done right away, World War Three will happen. I'm sure of it. I have no control. It doesn't take long at all.

Plus, it's fun, and—oh my goodness—the feeling is absolutely amazing. It makes the risk that much easier to bear. I've done this a ton of times, probably close to a million. (Well, maybe not that much, but a lot.) It's pretty much routine at this point.

I don't think I'm breaking any rules—probably just a huge gasp of embarrassment if someone sees me. My self-esteem is pretty high, though, so even that wouldn't be painful.

No one's around, but I check my surroundings a couple more times before starting.

What was I so scared of? If it wasn't that bad of a thing to do, what was the big deal? I'll tell you. What I once called a release, I now call an addiction.

The big deal is that I was an addict.

Technology these days makes it too easy. Me, myself, and my iPhone were all I needed to get going. No other materials were necessary. Well, maybe a napkin or an old gym shirt.

That little computer that fit in the palm of my hand could access a multi-billion-dollar industry from the touch of my fingers. Picking and choosing was swift because the industry made their websites incredibly easy to find what you're into.

Millions of pages and hundreds of categories were available to find any type of video you wanted. Man, was it diverse. I've never once talked to someone who couldn't find what they were looking for on one of those websites.

For me, some days were different than others. My interests were not broad, but my mood dictated my interests. All that mattered was the amount of free time I had to find what I wanted. If I had a lot of time, I wouldn't settle for anything less than what I was in the mood for. On plenty of occasions, I'd spend an hour searching for something.

This embarrasses me now.

If I didn't have a lot of time, I'd settle and get it over with. Despite the same shameful and guilt-ridden feelings that consumed me at the end of whatever I'd picked, it still felt good.

But why didn't I ever care about how it made me feel afterwards? Was it not bad? Or did I just not care what it was doing to my soul?

If you haven't guessed by now what I'm talking about, you're in good hands. You haven't been around it or experienced it, let alone performed what was necessary to get addicted to it. That is a good thing.

Or are you just lying to yourself? Are you addicted as well?

Isn't it just crazy how no one talks about pornography? It might be the most addictive thing the world is doing, and there are barely any conversations about it.

As I'm typing this, I've been clean for over a year now. *Clean*? Isn't that a term used for druggies? Porn is just as powerful as a drug. It's addicting, it ruins your brain, and it wreaks havoc on your relationships.

Sound familiar? Hopefully, by the time you read this, I'll be years and years into being clean from porn because I will never forget two things: I was addicted to porn for almost two decades, and that I was born again. Jesus is the only way.

I can honestly say that such an addiction takes a lot of skill and great ability to lie about it.

Men need help. Pornography is an addiction that should be treated like any other addiction: with support. Hopefully, someone will love you enough to sit down and talk openly about it. It's not just a "guy" thing, and it shouldn't be treated that way either. (Yes, girls are addicted to porn too).

I can clearly remember countless times, in every sexual relationship I was in, before Christ, I watched porn behind my partner's back. I watched at least every day, and I'm not even going to go into the times I did it multiple times a day.

Again, why didn't I care that I would ultimately, 100-percent upset my partner? Did I not care that a porn addiction ruins trust and destroys the capability of my partner to be good enough?

I thought, *Heck, who cares if she's ever good enough? If she's not good enough, I'll just relieve myself later with some video that has been watched over a million times.* I still can't believe that some of these porn videos have over a million views!

You want to know something scary about the insecurity of porn addiction? Most men won't agree with the thought of being *addicted* to porn. If they're not addicted, why don't the millions of us "non-addicted" guys get in one room and watch the video together?

If you aren't insecure about it, then you should have no problem with that idea. I sure in the heck didn't do that during my addiction. The addicted are insecure because they're addicted and don't want to admit to needing help.

I'm writing this in the hopes that I can broadcast to people that it's okay to have a problem, and that they should tell someone about it. Isn't that what we're on this planet to do? To help each other?

Did I think watching pornography gave me confidence to know what to do in bed? You betcha it did. Man, did I know all the tricks. I knew what spots to hit and what positions worked best. I knew everything in the bedroom, or bathroom, or truck, or anywhere, for that matter. I rocked.

If that sounds absolutely ridiculous to you, I couldn't agree more. What an egotistical thing to say! What's the point of knowing all the tricks if you don't even know how to make real love? What's the point of any of it if it goes against the fundamental teachings of the Gospel?

I'd say that once in about ten sexual encounters, whether I was in a relationship or not, I was making love and really enjoying the moment. The other nine experiences might as well have been porno, and I might as well have been an actor. Shoot, in my arrogant opinion, in some circumstances I *should've* gotten paid for my performance.

WHAT?!

How could I take something so special—an experience that's not just physical but emotional and spiritual—to such drastic and disgusting measures? It makes me want to throw up now.

The old me wanted so badly to brag to my friends about what I did. Far too often, I'd say something stupid like, "I bet she can't even walk."

I wasn't a man at all. I was a loser, and losers don't get far. They get dumped, and they get forgotten.

Okay, enough bashing on myself, but don't get me wrong. It's okay for me to make fun of myself. It's only okay because I feel like my outlook on pornography has completely changed, and it has. Lesson learned.

I don't have any desire to watch it now. I don't want to partake in sinful sexual activities whatsoever. That now goes completely against my faith; it goes against what the Bible teaches.

If I did it now, I'd let myself down, but more importantly, I'd let Jesus down. I'd be so disappointed if I chose to disrespect women to the fullest extent again.

More important than how I'd feel, it would be how my Heavenly Father would feel. I would disappoint the person I look up to the most. I am his son now, and I don't ever want that to change.

It's black and white. Follow Christ, and *everything* will fall into place the right way and at the right time.

I'm listening now. More importantly-

I'm following.

"If you love me, keep my commands. And I will ask the Father, and he will give you another advocate to help you and be with you forever— the Spirit of truth. The world cannot accept him, because it neither sees him nor knows him. But you know him, for he lives with you and will be in you."
(John 14:15-17 NIV)

CHAPTER 6

Therefore, as God's chosen people, holy and dearly loved, clothe yourselves with compassion, kindness, humility, gentleness and patience.
(Colossians 3:12)

EXILED

Yep, I was *that* kid.

The kid every parent doesn't want. The troublemaker. The "I don't care about getting suspended from school" kid. The one who wasn't necessarily a bully, but I wasn't necessarily nice either. I was the kid who got my family kicked out of the church. Maybe that's why it took me almost fifteen years to understand and to meet God again.

They put the kid who needed Jesus back out into a world that needs Jesus the most. I was isolated, and growing up in a dysfunctional family didn't help. I had a mom, a dad, and a twin brother.

Oh, wait. Did I mention that I had a half-sister I didn't know about until I was twenty-two years old? Who knows what kind of sin was lurking around my family throughout my childhood. I didn't know Christ, so I didn't know what was right or wrong.

Well, I kind of did. I knew what was okay and what wasn't. The problem was, though, I didn't care.

God bless my mother, because she definitely tried. She once tried to put my brother and I into a youth program.

She was a faithful volunteer at church. She did everything that was asked of her, and she did it with grace. It wasn't until they figured out that the kid who might as well have been the devil's offspring was in the youth program wreaking havoc.

"We got kicked out because of you," my mom would say with a chuckle. She laughs now, but when it happened it was the truth. Our church didn't want the Quilici family around. It was best if we left—especially after the cops and fire truck showed up at the church one night.

Nothing dangerous or crazy happened, but I was definitely the one who called the first responders to come help the ceiling.

Ceiling? Yeah.

Somehow, I thought it was cool to take all the sharpened pencils and throw them up into the ceiling until they got stuck. Once I was an accomplished pencil-thrower, I picked up the phone and didn't think twice while dialing the numbers 9-1-1.

"Nine-one-one... what's your emergency?" said the operator.

"Come quick! All the pencils are in the ceiling!" I yelled, then I hung up.

Cracking myself up I didn't really know what I had just done.

Sure enough, the sirens got closer and closer. Before I knew it, the cop cars and fire trucks came to a stop in the front of the church. At this point, my laughter turned into panic.

After it was all said and done... after figuring out that it was all just a silly prank, it disrupted church. What seemed to be only a few minutes later the leaders of the church asked us to leave. To be honest, we never went back, nor did I want to.

This is a simple story, and a funny one. I don't know if this was the reason why it took me so long to get back to Christ. I'm twenty-eight years old now. Had this church experience left a bitter taste in my mouth? This will definitely be a question I have for God when I go home.

What I didn't know or understand back then was how selfish I was. It hurts my heart knowing that I not only hurt my walk with the Lord as a junior high kid, it also had a huge impact on my twin brother's walk, because he didn't go back either. I know it's not right for me to take all the blame for my family's walk. I just didn't help.

I'm reminded of the Prodigal Son story in the Bible. Regardless how long it took me to meet God again, it didn't matter, because He loved me just as much:

The Parable of the Lost Son

[11] Jesus continued: "There was a man who had two sons. [12] The younger one said to his father, 'Father, give me my share of the estate.' So he divided his property between them.

[13] "Not long after that, the younger son got together all he had, set off for a distant country and there squandered his wealth in wild living. [14] After he had spent everything, there was a severe famine in that whole country, and he began to be in need. [15] So he went and hired himself out to a citizen of that country, who sent him to his fields to feed pigs. [16] He longed to fill his stomach with the pods that the pigs were eating, but no one gave him anything.

[17] "When he came to his senses, he said, 'How many of my father's hired servants have food to spare, and here I am starving to death! [18] I will set out and go back to my father and say to him: Father, I have sinned against heaven and against you. [19] I am no longer worthy to be called your son; make me like one of your hired servants.' [20] So he got up and went to his father.

"But while he was still a long way off, his father saw him and was filled with compassion for him; he ran to his son, threw his arms around him and kissed him.

[21] "The son said to him, 'Father, I have sinned against heaven and against you. I am no longer worthy to be called your son.'

[22] "But the father said to his servants, 'Quick! Bring the best robe and put it on him. Put a ring on his finger and sandals on his feet. [23] Bring the fattened calf and kill it. Let's have a feast and celebrate. [24] For this son of mine was dead and is alive again; he was lost and is found.' So they began to celebrate.

[25] "Meanwhile, the older son was in the field. When he came near the house, he heard music and dancing. [26] So he called one of the servants and asked him what was going on.[27] 'Your brother has come,' he replied, 'and your father has killed the fattened calf because he has him back safe and sound.'

[28] "The older brother became angry and refused to go in. So his father went out and pleaded with him. [29] But he answered his father, 'Look! All these years I've been slaving for you and never disobeyed your orders. Yet you never gave me even a young goat so I could celebrate with my friends. [30] But when this son of yours who has squandered your property with prostitutes comes home, you kill the fattened calf for him!'

[31] "'My son,' the father said, 'you are always with me, and everything I have is yours. [32] But we had to celebrate and be glad, because this brother of yours was dead and is alive again; he was lost and is found.'"

Luke 15:11-32 NIV

CHAPTER 7

"Your beauty should not come from outward adornment, such as elaborate hairstyles and the wearing of gold jewelry or fine clothes. Rather, it should be that of your inner self, the unfading beauty of a gentle and quiet spirit, which is of great worth in God's sight."
(1 Peter 3:3–4 NIV)

SMITTEN

A cowlick is the best way of describing the little curl of hair right at the top of her forehead. It made her bangs naturally longer, and, honestly, made it insanely easy for her to wake up every morning looking exactly like she'd gone to bed. "Luck," she called it.

She had what most girls wanted to replicate: a beautiful, curly flow of gorgeous brown hair without her even having to do anything to it. I could *swear* that she had hints of actual gold in her hair.

Sometimes, it seemed like she'd gotten up in the middle of the night to curl her hair just to play a trick on me. Nope. It was just her gift. Don't even get me started about when she had time to actually do something to it. I'd think, *No way could she look any better.* But man, was I wrong.

I know I'm talking about hair, but it was hers, and I loved every strand.

❧

Her brown eyes were the highlight of every smile she gave

me. When she laughed at someone else for no particular reason, I got jealous of that person. They were stealing my smile.

I wanted all of them. They made my heart happy. Her smile was the easiest way for me to smile. Even when I was down, those smiles were contagious, especially when her cheeks were as big as hot air balloons. (We'd ridden in one together, by the way.)

She had what she called a problem: one cheek had a missing dimple. How the heck does that happen? She must've smiled too much and one of her hot-air-balloon cheeks popped. That's my theory. Call it stupid, but in return, I'll call you crazy.

I loved that missing dimple.

There's nothing that can drop a man to his knees like a woman's stunning smile. But on some days, whatever it may be, a fight, a slip of words, I'd see that smile turn to a frown and tears flow from those golden-brown eyes. It was in those moments that I realized what kind of man I really was.

Did I call her a weak person who couldn't handle her emotions? Or was I there for her, sympathizing with her, and making her feelings more important than mine?

I'll give you one big fat guess which kind of man I was.

This chapter doesn't have a particular story behind it; I was a jerk too many times to pinpoint just ONE memory. I was selfish. I didn't care about feelings other than my own. I knew what the foundation of this relationship had been built upon: physical attraction.

I love the "love at first sight" idea, but if you don't have a firm foundation of Christ in you, the understanding of inward beauty is lost. Without it the relationship will eventually die—especially when you get older and wrinkles start happening. That's when you may wish you'd made different life choices.

God has taught me a lot, but two things stick out... I must care about placing others' feelings before mine and recognizing how beautiful someone's soul can be. If tears are coming, it's time for empathy first and opinion later. I don't care who you are: the last thing anybody wants when they're down is advice on how to feel better and to stop crying.

Rid the word *need* from your vocabulary. "You need to do this. You need to go there. You need to fill your schedule. You need to eat."

Those are all examples of advice at the wrong time. When someone is sad or heartbroken, all you need to do is be there and offer comfort.

Empathy and presence is critical. In my world, this is also known as a dang hug. Or maybe a simple "I'm sorry" can do the trick.

Oh yeah, knucklehead: actually mean it.

I'm reminded of Philippians 2:1–7: "*Therefore if you have any encouragement from being united with Christ, if any comfort from his love, if any common sharing in the Spirit, if any tenderness and compassion, then make my joy complete by being like-minded, having the same love, being one in spirit and of one mind. Do nothing out of selfish ambition or vain conceit. Rather, in humility value others above yourselves, not looking to your own interests but each of you to the interests of the others." (NIV)*

You need to quell your selfish feelings. Whatever the situation is, if you hurt someone's feelings, own it.

Be more like Jesus. It takes a lot of courage to sit there and humble yourself to an emotion you don't necessarily agree with, but over time your agreement with that feeling will get easier.

Just try not to make anybody cry. Be brave, and remember: Put others' feelings in front of your own.

Husbands, love your wives and do not be harsh with them.
(Colossians 3:19 NIV)

CHAPTER 8

"A new command I give you: Love one another. As I have loved you, so you must love one another. By this everyone will know that you are my disciples, if you love one another." (John 13:34-35 NIV)

STUNTED

Match her effort.
Respect her hustle.
Support her ambition.
Protect her heart.
Value her loyalty.
Uplift her spirit.
Love her unconditionally.
How?
Jesus Christ.

If she writes a book about her life, I have a title she should use: *Short and Strong*.

When I first met her, I obviously knew she was physically short, but it didn't take me long to figure out how emotionally powerful she was. And man, was she athletic! Growing up, she played all kinds of sports, but one stood out that blew my mind: stunting, which stems from the cheerleading world. It's an understatement to say how much sheer strength is required to stunt, or at least be the best at it, which she was.

You think I would've dated someone who wasn't athletic? That'd be embarrassing! (I like reminding you how much of a jerk I was.) Anyways. She was a flyer in the sport of cheerleading. Oh, are you one of those people who just now wondered if I said cheerleading was a sport? Well, I'm glad you can read. Cheerleading is easily one of the coolest *sports*.

Cheerleading is pretty much the most important part of any sporting event. They inspire you to root for your team and get you fired up, even when all hope seems lost. Of course, they were all pretty impressive to look at. The beauty of every single one of the cheerleaders on her squad was nothing short of amazing.

Maybe you've seen girls get thrown into the air and do tricks. They're tossed up with no signs of fear, and they land on their partners' (usually male) hands in complete and full balance—like nothing extraordinary had just happened. What incredible strength and coordination it takes to stay tight and straight enough for someone to catch and hold them ten feet off the ground and not think twice about it.

All sorts of tricks are available to a stunt duo, from full ups (complete 360s) to rewinds (backflips), to you-name-it. Risking lives just to keep the crowd entertained! What sacrifice. The next time you see a sporting event, make sure you watch these girls.

Her partner would grab her by the waist, throw her up in the air, and with his arm fully extended, catch her with one hand. He might as well have been called Hercules, but his job was easy compared to hers. Did I mention that I had been a stuntman for a year? Way harder than it looks.

Her job was *trust*. She had to trust him with everything she had. Her life was on the line. She had to trust that he would successfully complete the stunt. If he didn't, she had to trust him enough to catch her safely after the failed attempt.

That was just in regard to her jumping straight up. Imagine her fear when she decided it was time to do a complete flip before he caught her. (He was so blessed to have a super-strong, athletic, and patient teaching partner; she was one of the best in the business.)

Can you imagine risking your life doing something you had *zero* control over? Give them a round of applause! What courage! What strength!

Speaking of power, she was one of the very few on the team who lifted weights and took working out seriously. She wasn't just a cheerleader; she was an athlete. She did everything so well, from learning new techniques to new sports. Long story short, she was a natural at *everything*. She even joined the sport of Olympic Weightlifting, which requires an insane amount of technique and athleticism in order to be competitive.

Olympic Weightlifting revolves around two lifts, the snatch and the clean and jerk. The snatch consists of getting a weight over your head in one motion. The clean and jerk consists of getting the most weight overhead in two movements. The only difference is that in the clean and jerk you get a break halfway. So, in theory, you can lift more weight.

For both events, it's just you and a barbell. You have to trust and allow yourself to be completely underneath weight that can crush you. Dropping the barbell in an unlearned fashion can cause serious injury. Understand something for me please: this sport is in the *Olympics,* and people work their *entire* lives to have a chance to win a gold medal. So the fear factor cannot be there.

Having a personality that trusts your personal strength is hard to come by. This girl had enough strength and courage to walk away from something (me) that wasn't healthy, a relationship where happiness was nowhere to be found. She was strong, fearless, and most importantly, hard-working.

I loved her, but I didn't love her for her abilities. When we were together, I didn't appreciate how awesome she was. Like, come on: How many women get thrown into the air and also willingly throw around weight in the gym, but are also caring, compassionate, generous, selfless, and incredibly loving?

If you have a special person in your life, look at my poor recognition skills and understand that appreciation of the little things goes a long way.

If you give your whole life to Jesus, he will open it and transform it. He will give you the ability to love like never before. He will be the Heavenly Father you never had, telling you, "Give heartfelt compliments and appreciate others' beauty."

Husbands, in the same way be considerate as you live with your wives, and treat them with respect as the weaker partner and as heirs with you of the gracious gift of life, so that nothing will hinder your prayers.
(1 Peter 3:7 NIV)

CHAPTER 9

"So let God work his will in you. Yell a loud no to the Devil and watch him scamper. Say a quiet yes to God and he'll be there in no time. Quit dabbling in sin. Purify your inner life. Quit playing the field. Hit bottom, and cry your eyes out. The fun and games are over. Get serious, really serious. Get down on your knees before the Master; it's the only way you'll get on your feet."
(James 4:7–10 MSG)

PUSHED

Let's point out the elephant in the room: Did you honestly think someone like me could sit down and pour my feelings out without a girl being involved?

I knew you were a funny one.

Yes, of course there was a girl.

She ripped my heart out.

Or did I rip out my own—pulling it out of my chest with calloused, selfish hands, wondering why she was gone? Did I have my barely pumping, dripping heart in my hand, wondering who I was going to throw it at so I could blame my suicidal thoughts on someone other than me? After all, I didn't realize how self-centered I was until we broke up.

There's nothing like putting the blame on someone else. How could *I* do something wrong? I'm way too cool for that.

I don't like pie—not pumpkin pie, apple pie, or any pie. I'm the guy who gets a *ton* of weird looks on Thanksgiving, the greatest pie day of the year. Their judgmental eyes say, "C'mon! Who *doesn't* have a piece of pie on this fantastic holiday?"

I'm more of an ice-cream-paired-with-a-bunch-of-chocolate-chip-cookies guy. (There better be ice cream in heaven, or else I don't want to go.)

I did discover what kind of pie I liked when it was shoved down my throat: the worst-tasting pie there is... humble pie. It's hard to swallow, especially when you have an ego the size of a football stadium. With each bite, tears. With each swallow, rage. With each piece devoured, regret. I didn't even have any dang whipped cream to dull the taste. It hurt. It hurt a lot.

Let's just say that this beautiful lady brought me back to earth.

Don't get me wrong. In every relationship, it goes both ways, but—wow—did I *not* do my part. But did we both learn valuable lessons? I'm sure, but it didn't just teach me things; it changed my life.

She pushed me to be better, but I didn't see it. I didn't understand it. I didn't agree with it. I didn't need any help—with anything. I had it all figured out. I knew what I wanted, and I was well on my way. I was just lucky enough to have her as a gorgeous tagalong. She might as well have been my sidekick who occasionally gave me a kiss.

Man, was I an idiot.

Now, stop right there.

If you already think this is a "feel sorry for me" story, you have it all wrong. She led me to God. That saved my life. I can see that now.

It took me a while not to blame her for almost killing me, but she taught me a super valuable lesson: you can kill yourself, slowly, every day you think about yourself and only yourself. You lose, and you lose badly. Every piece of your soul and your heart slowly turns to stone.

I lost the game. I lost the battle. But she gave me a second chance to win the war we call life. It's heartbreaking to see the love of your life walk away and give up on you. But what's more heartbreaking is to stay with someone who's a jerk. The person who will someday break your heart if they remain on the path of selfishness. The heartbreak hurt, and it hurt a lot. But I'll take that heartbreak any day. My life has forever changed because of her.

I've realized the truth of my selfishness, and Galatians says it well:

"It is obvious what kind of life develops out of trying to get your own way all the time: repetitive, loveless, cheap sex; a stinking accumulation of mental and emotional garbage; frenzied and joyless grabs for happiness; trinket gods; magic-show religion; paranoid loneliness; cutthroat competition; all-consuming-yet-never-satisfied wants; a brutal temper; an impotence to love or be loved; divided homes and divided lives; small-minded and lopsided pursuits; the vicious habit of depersonalizing everyone into a rival; uncontrolled and uncontrollable addictions; ugly parodies of community. I could go on. This isn't the first time I have warned you, you know. If you use your freedom this way, you will not inherit God's kingdom" (Galatians 5:19–21, MSG).

Kissing her feet? This book isn't about me trying to win her heart back. This is about giving the person who led me to God some light. In all regards, I know she mostly did this for her reasons, but any decision that affects a relationship has a ripple effect. It just so happened that the ripple effect led me to God.

But if we're going to be real, she might as well have been the one who pushed me to my death over an endless cliff of a dark abyss, falling and falling with no sign of stopping, no sign of sunshine or hope. The death of my old self.

But you know who saved my life. My main man, Jesus.

Most of you who vomit at love stories and can't stand sitting in a movie theater watching a romantic comedy probably think, "Finally! That's over."

Sorry to break it to you. How can I put the love of my life in a book without explaining to everyone how we met?

I know: you're super excited. Don't you just love you some love?

More importantly, relationships are probably going to be the most genuine and heartfelt parts of your life. The biggest and most important relationship is with God, of course.

If you're unable to open up about your heartbreaks and pain, then you have a lot to learn.

So, yes. This next part of my book is all about how we met. Which was, for me at least, love at first sight.

It's important to know what real love feels like—graceful love, love that is unconditional, unexplainable, unimaginable, *agape* love from your Lord and Savior Jesus Christ. When love happens with another human again, you'll be ready, and you'll do it right. You will know how to love because you know *who* love is.

You aren't alone in heartbreak town. Just let the world know and be okay with the fact that you screwed up. I promise, admitting it will feel fantastic. Just be understanding of what *not* to do next time, and, duh: don't drink too much.

Love never gives up.
Love cares more for others than for self.
Love doesn't want what it doesn't have.
Love doesn't strut,
Doesn't have a swelled head,
Doesn't force itself on others,
Isn't always "me first,"
Doesn't fly off the handle,
Doesn't keep score of the sins of others,
Doesn't revel when others grovel,
Takes pleasure in the flowering of truth,
Puts up with anything,
Trusts God always,
Always looks for the best,
Never looks back,
But keeps going to the end.
(1 Corinthians 13:3–7 MSG)

CHAPTER 10

"For everything in the world—the lust of the flesh, the lust of the eyes, and the pride of life—comes not from the Father but from the world."
(1 John 2:16 NIV)

KISSED

A "fresh" start with the same habits, the same selfish ways, and without God, is just stupid.

I learned that after I finally made it out of the frat house. Two years of living there, with endless partying and trying to have as much "fun" as possible, was unbelievably exhausting. I needed a fresh start. I needed to move on.

It was a blessing to have a great friend, who was also a brother in the fraternity house, living in a "regular" house not far from campus. To this day, I wonder why I cared to still be close to campus. It wasn't like I cared about my grades or my degree at that point. I must have still wanted to be close to the party scene. Who knows? The only skill I took away from college was how to chug a beer faster than anybody else. I still don't understand why I had to be the best at everything back in the day. That was exhausting too.

This "regular" house had three girls who lived in it before my buddy and I moved in. What a score: moving in with some chicks! Yee-haw.

Wait a minute. It gets better: they were *cheerleaders*!

Is that what I needed? To surround myself with more of

what I honestly thought I was trying to get away from? All I could truthfully reflect on during that time was whether the girls I was going to live with were hot or not. (As if they *weren't* going to be pretty—it seemed obvious. Come on! They were cheerleaders! Jaw drop, fist pump, chest pump, do 50 pushups. Why 50? Because 'Merica! Salute to the states! Then chug a beer. Boom.)

Well, I guessed right. They were attractive, and above all else, they were relaxed and welcoming. There's nothing like living with beautiful women walking around in their cheerleading outfits.

I was in heaven, or so I thought.

❧

One of the girls shouted, "We're going to throw a housewarming party and invite all the girls over."

I wondered why she was yelling until I realized that's what she was born to do. After living with those girls for almost a week, I was pretty much deaf, but that was okay. It was the weekend, and it was time to get excited and meet all the pretty ladies.

The night started calmly, and the female-to-male ratio was excellent. There were probably ten girls for every guy. Now that's what I'm talking about! I had endless conversations about how much I worked out and didn't study. I was always a people person, and I can carry a conversation for days, even if we're talking about dolphins. I was typical Zack: flirting up a storm, chugging beers, and just enjoying the moment.

Suddenly, an short girl walks in.

I sensed her energy, like she wanted to be the life of the party as much as I did. I accomplished that with my voice and jokes and making sure everyone had what they needed so they could have a good time at my house. She did it with her smile, her beauty, and simply having the noticeably biggest heart in the room. You could sense that she honestly cared about people.

Her presence made me momentarily change who I was. I suddenly didn't care about anything or anyone but this short girl. She had the power to stop me in my tracks and make me instantly forget how to talk. I may have asked my roommate who she was, but my words came out entirely different. Being drunk didn't help.

I probably said something like, "Her, yeah. That one. I'd like to share my Lucky Charms cereal with her."

Saying something that ridiculous confirmed two things: I loved Lucky Charms too much, and yet I was willing to share mine with this beautiful girl. She might as well have been the leprechaun to my Lucky Charms.

Anyway, I fell in love.

I didn't get the chance to talk to her much that night, but I got her name, and she made a lasting impression on me while making the whole party laugh with her jokes. It wasn't long until I figured out her full name, so I could stalk her on social media. Facebook is such an awesome invention.

Eventually, I did what most courageous and brave men do to land a date with a girl: I messaged her on Facebook. Man, was it hard to press that send button. In my era, it is the most nerve-racking first step toward a relationship. The thought of my full heart going into a simple Facebook message was a tough one, especially since I didn't know if she would even respond! In fact, I didn't even press send; I had my roommate do it.

I checked my phone every thirty seconds after that. I wanted her so badly to respond. My message said, "Hey! Tomorrow my fraternity has a huge beer pong tournament and dance party, and I need a date/partner! I was wondering if you wanted to join?"

Beer pong. How romantic.

FYI: beer pong is a beer-drinking "sport" involving ping-pong balls and red cups. In other words, it's a way to get super drunk tossing balls around. (If you need more help understanding the foundation of contemporary Greek life, Google is your best friend.)

Our frat knew that we could use the co-ed tournament as a scapegoat for actually planning a date with a girl. It was easy: Ask a girl to come. If she says no, ask the next one. Whenever I'd ask a girl to come to a fraternity event, I'd receive a yes ten out of ten times. Fist pump. Honestly, I didn't care about the event as much as I cared about this one short girl positively responding to my invitation.

I knew that I'd fallen in love and wanted more than just a beer pong partner. I wanted to squeeze her until her cute little head popped off. I was secretly obsessed. Time lasted an eternity while I waited for a notification to pop up from this girl. I wanted to see her beautiful name. I wanted to get to know her. How could these emotions be so powerful when I'd just met her? Is love at first sight even possible?

When she responded, "Yes! Soooo down :)," my life forever changed.

I somehow had a good feeling about this one.

For the tournament, we had to match. We had to be, act, and communicate as a team. We were going into battle for a prestigious title: "The Champs." I don't even think there was a trophy. (Too much beer?) Winning was all that mattered in my life then, so I hoped she was bringing her A-game.

As an immature frat guy, I chose a respectable team theme. We showed up as "Thugs," probably because I just wanted to wear a tank top to show off my huge biceps to the future love of my life. I even had Nerf guns to put in my waistline. I wish I could show you pictures of how ridiculous we looked.

We were in a huge bracket with around fifty teams. It was about to get real—just like the love and excitement I felt for this girl I didn't even know yet.

Just as the tournament was about to begin, I asked myself, "Where is she?" Desperately hoping she hadn't flaked out on me, I finally got a message saying, "I think I'm here." Apparently, she'd gotten lost because it was her first time at the frat house.

How could I be mad? I was about thirty-four beers deep already (frat guy skills), and the most beautiful girl at the party had finally arrived with an awesome shirt on: it read "Thug Life." I wish I could explain how funny and cute it was that this little, short girl was trying to be a gangster. She did have good aim though. I remember perfectly well that she shot one Nerf dart right into my eye.

We lost the tournament, but I didn't care. Win or lose, I'd still won. I woke up the next day feeling like a million bucks. Or was I still drunk? Either way, I had a crush, and I was crushing hard. I couldn't explain how I felt. I'm not that funny of a guy, but when she laughed with me all night, I knew that a chance for love could happen. Had she been laughing that I had a fake black teardrop below my eye, artistically and strategically drawn with makeup to make my "thug" outfit more pathetic? Maybe it was the gold chain from the dollar store. Who knows?

What I do know is that any girl who was willing to deal with a frat party, let alone a frat guy like me, and still maintain her sense of pride, got points on my scoreboard. She didn't try to act like someone else. She knew her limits, and she had fun within them. This girl, this beautiful, beautiful girl—I had to have her.

❧

I'm going to save you some time: we fell in love, and we fell in love quickly. We complemented each other so well and our conversations never lacked chemistry. Our text messages were *novels*. It wasn't until I asked her best friend for advice that I soon realized the girl of my dreams thought that I didn't like her!

Oh, *heck* no. I had to clear that up real quick and make her my girlfriend as soon as possible. If anything in life is hard, it's the beginning of a possible relationship: what to say, when to say it, blah blah blah. Girls are confusing to guys, and guys have a problem with saying how they really feel. Apparently, I suffered from that. How could I have been in love with someone while she thinks that I don't even like her? Whatever, I sucked it up and made moves —quick.

Kickoff for our college's homecoming game against Wyoming was 4:05 p.m. on October 6, 2012. And because themes seemed to follow us, it was superhero night. But all I thought about that day was how I was going to ask her out. What was I going to say? I knew that if I could get *one* minute of her time before the game I was going to do it.

Since she was a cheerleader, she was in the team room discussing pregame details and routines, but wow, did I get lucky. She was able to text me while I walked through the middle of campus to get to the game. My heart was exploding with adrenaline and excitement. I calmed down with a few beers, because, yeah, beer makes everything better.

I'd argue that this was the most nauseated I've felt in my whole life. I was about to arrive at the ticket gate to enter the stadium, but right before the gate, there it was: the team room, the room where the most amazing girl I had ever seen would hopefully see my text and just pop out for a few seconds before she made her way to the game to perform. People were all around, and I was with a couple of best friends. The environment of this college football game was electric. Nobody was in a bad mood. It was game day, let alone homecoming. Everyone was smiling from ear to ear.

The smell of hot dogs and burgers was in the air, as well as the aroma of a late autumn afternoon. What a perfect day. It was around 3:30 when I sent the text, "Hey, come outside for a second. I'm at the team room." After a few moments, I got a text back saying, "Okay, but I only have a few minutes, don't make fun of my socks."

Now I'm shaking. It's about to happen. The thought of this had really built up. Having those beers before-hand was obviously a bad "calming" method. It didn't work at all.

I didn't really understand the whole sock thing until she came out. Her beautiful smile stopped me in my tracks. Now I'm about to pass out. I immediately gave her a hug when she walked up, followed by a glance down to her wonderfully funny outfit. Because it was superhero night, she had to wear knee-high socks that had a cute, little Superman cape attached to the socks. A cape on socks? Sweet, right?

I turned back to her and looked her right in the eyes while holding her hands. I'm sure she felt me shaking uncontrollably. I mumbled, "I like you a lot. I really do, and I'm wondering if you'd be my girlfriend?"

Without hesitation, she said yes. I felt my soul explode with genuine happiness. I picked her up from underneath her arms, with both of her arms going around my neck. She was flying. Her cape socks became ironic; now she was now two feet off the ground and looking right at me, eye-level.

We kissed.

I said, "You just made me the happiest man alive."

I didn't want the moment to end, but I knew that she had to get back to her teammates inside. I gave her another kiss, and she ran back. I think I saw a few bunny skips of happiness. With one look back at me from inside, she waved and blew me a kiss.

That was the beginning of the most loving and life-changing relationship I've ever been in.

❧

Have you heard the term "Power Couple"? If not, let me explain.

If our relationship was a puzzle, we would be the last two pieces to complete it: the best pieces, the pieces that *everyone* wanted to put in place, the ones that allowed you to take a deep breath and enjoy the overwhelming feeling of accomplishment—the best feeling in the world at that moment.

But I know now that our puzzle was a disaster, with missing pieces, pieces eaten by the dog, pieces that got wet from too much beer, and most importantly, pieces that had been put in place the way *I* wanted.

We were *it*. We complemented each other to the moon and back. If there was a flaw of mine that people noticed (as if the opinions of others mattered to me then), she would make up for it, and vice- versa. We were good-looking as well as overly helpful.

I saw us as the couple everyone dreamed of being, the epitome of every good relationship. We sparked a light in each room we walked into. People always wanted us around. Most of the time, we'd always make any situation better, a trip more fun, and a party more vibrant. If we weren't there, everyone would ask where we were. We were *it*.

People were already asking us for invitations to the wedding. Man, was *that* going to be a celebration of this dreamy power couple or what! We were already talking about what we would name our kids when we had some! Being the exact definition of a fairytale was easy to uphold. It came naturally for us. We both were big personalities with an overall goal of just loving everyone we met.

We seemed to have everything together: we were both in college, and then we decided to open a CrossFit gym together. Boom! What a power couple! We were perfect, attractive, friendly, athletic, and, to top it off, we opened a business. What can get any better than that?

Nothing. I had it made. I had and did anything I wanted. Who needs God if you have the perfect girl, perfect business, and perfect life?

Then, after a few years Jesus said, "*What about me?*"

R RELYING ON GOD'S WORD
E ENCOURAGING AND BUILDING EACH OTHER UP
L LONG-LASTING
A ALWAYS BE PATIENT
T TELLING THEM THEY ARE BEAUTIFUL AS THEY ARE
I I TRUST IN GOD AND YOU
O ONE THAT IS CHRIST CENTERED
N NEVER LEAD EACH OTHER ASTRAY FROM JESUS
S SEEKING GOD FIRST
H HUMBLE YOURSELF BEFORE EVERYONE
I I AM COMMITTED TO LOVING YOU
P PRAY FOR EACH OTHER
S SHARE THE WORD WITH EACH OTHER

-UNKNOWN

CHAPTER 11

"You shall not steal."

(Exodus 20:15)

STOLEN

You know that feeling you get when stealing second base? The jump, the first few steps, and all the fast-twitch muscles you need to get to the bag before the catcher has a chance to throw you out? *One* bad step, and you're out.

You never know when you're going to get another shot to be on first base again. So, you have to give your all on this ninety-feet of pure sprint. *One* shot, one slide, and hopefully you're looking at the ump yelling, "Safe!"

But you might get a call in the game of life that could wreck your world, wreck the fact that your first step toward second was way too slow. You let yourself down. You let your team down. But the funny thing is, we learn at a very young age to forgive ourselves and to have a short memory in sports.

The next time you're at bat and you get lucky enough to try to steal second base again, you might remember what happened the last time. Then one of two things will happen: you'll try harder, dig your cleats into the ground until your legs give out. You gave 100 percent effort the last time; now it's time for 150 percent.

Or, you might be so resentful of your last performance that it's going to screw up everything on your at bats to come. And heck, who knows, you might never see first base again (especially if you keep that resentful attitude). Suck it up, buttercup! It's OK. Let it go.

You try again. "Safe!" yells the umpire. From those four letters, your last memory of being called out is instantly forgotten.

That's why so many sports players grow up with a great character base. We learn to have a short memory when something doesn't go our way.

Why is it so hard for adults to do that?

I understand that baseball is a game, and life isn't. You eventually have to just wash your uniform and put it on again.

❧

Long story short: remember the gym that I opened with my ex? When I got dumped I went crazy and did enough partying to put the gym into debt. After a few months of being reckless, the only option was to sell it.

I might not get another opportunity to open a business, but does that mean I'm going to forgive myself? Or should I wallow in utter disgust that I once opened a business but ended up in a bottomless pit of disappointment?

Or is this God's way of showing me who he is?

As to opening the gym, let's just say I didn't do it the right way. In my eyes, I stole it. I didn't do anything illegal, but it was definitely breaking the moral law. We will get to that soon.

❧

"CrossFit is constantly varied functional movements performed at high intensity. All CrossFit workouts are based on functional movements, and these movements reflect the best aspects of gymnastics, weightlifting, running, rowing and more."

What an awesome sport. CrossFit was another avenue for us washed-up athletes to have fun still competing in a friendly and camaraderie-filled atmosphere. Going to CrossFit workouts felt like I was strapping on my football cleats again every time I walked in the door. I wanted to do it every day, so I considered the possibility of becoming a coach.

I forked over the thousand bucks and drove my butt all the way up to Boise, Idaho. If you know anything about me, I'm an impulse-driven person. So, I was *all in* when this happened. I even skipped a couple of months' rent just to pay for my trip and the class. I was a weekend away from being a CrossFit trainer.

CrossFit is the best way to get in shape, period—well, at least for the people who suck at working out alone. Ninety percent of the time, people don't know what to do to get started in the fitness world. They go to their local gym where all they do is take your money. You walk in without a clue what you're doing or how any of the machines work. It's a headache.

But CrossFit takes care of you right from the get-go. Think of it this way: CrossFit is like a one-on-one personal training session with a certified coach, but it's one-on-ten, and it's awesome!

People are scared of doing exercises wrong and getting embarrassed, but in CrossFit, you get instant feedback from your coach, who corrects, motivates, and inspires you, all in one sentence. You'll hear, "Great job! Let's keep that back straight! You are going to get so strong, so fast."

It's a great way to stay motivated and committed. Not only do you have a coach keeping you accountable, but you end up building awesome relationships with the other members of the gym. That often leads to a text message from your fellow classmates: "That workout was tough, are you going tomorrow?" Talk about fitness awesomeness.

❧

I always was good at relationships, especially when I became a coach. I cared about people's days and lives almost more than I cared about their fitness, which led to me having an incredible relationship with the owner of the gym I worked at.

He was such an incredible blessing. He opened the doors for me as a coach, and I started my fitness career under a watchful and diligent eye. He may have cared about me more than I cared about him. Actually, when I think about it, I don't think I cared about him at all.

I showed up on time every day and cared about "my" members and my selfish well-being all the time. I might have already thought to myself that I could run this place better than he could. I considered myself more of a people person than he was, so building strong and honest relationships with members was definitely easy for me. I'm not saying he wasn't a people person, but I was crazy in love with my job and the people. That allowed me to get up at 4:30 a.m. and motivate them.

Then the opportunity to ruin someone's life came.

Long story short, the owner of the gym went through some personal stuff. He asked me to cover more and more shifts while he was figuring things out. It got to the point where he wouldn't show up all day.

I jumped in the air with excitement at the time. I knew

that being the guy who opened and closed the gym was the beginning of taking on more leadership at the gym. It was a plus (as I crossed my fingers) because, again, I knew that I could do it better than he could.

His depression and lack of communication started to really frustrate me. He stopped paying me *and* stopped showing up. He even went weeks without showing his face at the business he owned. I didn't understand, so I started voicing my frustrations to our members. With affirmation from one of my most respectable clients—"You don't even need him"—I knew it was "Go" time.

About a month later, he started to show his face again, but he came back with some awesome news. He wasn't feeling any better, but he wanted to make me the "manager" of the gym.

It was a surreal feeling—I knew that this place was going to be mine. That's all I wanted. I didn't care what he was going through. I even remember saying to the members that it would be better when he was gone. He was a far better coach than me, but I wasn't the depressed one.

My life would be forever changed after I saw his car at the gym one day, at a time when it usually wasn't there.

❧

I walked into the gym about an hour before the next class started. He was sitting at his desk, crying. The man who'd given me this awesome opportunity, the dorkiest and funniest man I've ever met, was crying. He said, "There's no money anywhere. People are leaving. I'm a wreck, and I think I want to sell the place. What do you think?"

He was honestly asking me as a friend. He needed help deciding what to do. He trusted me. He loved me. I was his saving grace to help him through this awful time. My adrenaline shot through the roof. My hands shook. I knew what this meant: this was my time to shine. Screw him. *Sucks to suck*, I said in my head.

I quickly blurted out that he should think about selling it to me. I didn't have the money or the experience, but I knew I had an opportunity. After about thirty minutes of talking, I reversed the way I felt about buying it. I realized that it was impossible for me to come up with the necessary cash. So, it was time for Plan B: be a jerk and take advantage of this poor man.

I started gossiping to everyone. When he wasn't around, my goal was to tell as many members as I could about his thoughts of selling the gym. I began to receive emails and texts asking questions and wondering if the rumors were true. I couldn't help but spark their interest about me taking over as the owner, or, better yet, opening my own gym. Because, heck, this place was doomed.

I didn't want to help him through his nightmare; I just wanted to punish him more for "trusting me." It got bad, even to the point of him getting emails and texts about what was going on around the gym. Believe it or not, not everyone had my back. There were still some members who ultimately cared for the owner and his well-being.

One day, he came raging into the gym. I remember hearing his car come to a screeching halt. Right in the middle of me teaching a class, he told the class he was sorry for interrupting.

The class was mostly comprised of veteran CrossFitters, so they pretty much knew what they were doing. He politely asked if he could steal me for a quick meeting in his office.

I sat there as a pathological liar. Right to his face, I told lie after lie about the rumors *I* was personally and undoubtedly spreading. I'm a good actor.

"You believe me or the members? I would never do that to you man!" Blah blah blah. "I got your back." "Let's forget that this ever happened."

He was low. He was vulnerable. He was in a place where he trusted me. He gave me a hug and said, "Thank you, Zack. Thank you for keeping this gym afloat while I'm dealing with this."

Little did he know what I'd done: complete betrayal. It was unbelievable dishonesty, and I thought nothing of it. I pretty much said to myself *Good job* and *Phew, that was close*. What a jerk. Who would do such a thing to another human being, and especially to this guy who'd put his blood, sweat, and tears into this place? I'd had nothing to do with the foundation or the building of this business. I was just the guy kicking a man while he was down.

After a weekend of sleeping in, it was a typical Monday morning. I showed up around 5:30 to coach my morning class that started at 6 a.m. I was met with a lovely note on the door in the owner's handwriting: "Closed."

I quickly opened the door to find the office completely empty: no desk, no computer, none of the furniture. It was all gone. I remember a vacuum being left there. I panicked a little bit, knowing people were going to show up any minute. You already know that I cared about the members more than I cared about what happened to the owner.

I turned the corner, switched on the lights, then dropped my jaw and my coffee all in one motion. The gym was gutted. The owner must have done it over the weekend. He must have found out I was a liar.

I couldn't believe it, and I didn't understand how he'd done it so fast! But, again, I'd be a liar if I didn't tell you the truth: I was happy. I was thrilled that someone had lost their mind enough to do something like this, leaving seventy members without a gym to work out in.

I told people that he'd finally given up, without any thought of what I had done to him. It was all his fault, what with the way he couldn't handle his emotions. And leaving an entire business in the hands of a twenty-three-year-old was idiotic. He probably couldn't face me after he'd found out that my gossip was true. He must have bailed.

It only took me three months to open my own facility right around the corner. I was constantly emailing the group of people who'd been part of the gym that closed. They were all excited to join me. It was all perfect—opening a business that had a chance to have members sign up on day one was unthinkable. Little did I expect to see fifty people show up when I opened my gym.

Man, I must've been a great coach. People stayed with me. They followed me wherever I went. What loyalty. Dang—I must've been a great *guy*. With integrity like mine, I could see nothing other than success as long as I faithfully cared about my members and gave them a chance to be fit. Who cared how I got the gym open? Who cared what I did?

But the sacrifice of another human being's happiness to attain happiness myself is disgusting. For a long time, I didn't think I ever deserved to get another at bat, let alone to try to steal second base again.

Excuse me while I go to the bathroom to throw up. I've made myself sick.

When pride comes, then comes disgrace, but with humility comes wisdom.
(Proverbs 11:2 NIV)

CHAPTER 12

The Lord is not slow in keeping his promise, as some understand slowness. Instead he is patient with you, not wanting anyone to perish, but everyone to come to repentance.
(2 Peter 3:9)

SWATTED

On one memorable Saturday night, I was walking down the strip in Reno with two good friends and a friend of a friend. After a fun night of dancing and flirting, we did what every smart college kid did at three in the morning. We didn't want to get a DUI, so we took a short walk home instead.

It was about a fifteen-minute walk to my home at the fraternity house. We had walked to and from downtown plenty of times before, so this walk was routine.

But not this time.

As we walked past the Eldorado Casino, which ran for a good quarter-mile from stop light to stop light, we were lucky to be halfway in-between the outside of the casino.

Lucky? I'll explain later.

We were chatting about the night and making fun of ourselves because none of us were bringing a chick home. Back then, getting laid and getting some high fives were our top priority every night. Little did we know that we were soon going to be giving high fives to each other for a different reason.

Halfway down the block, two strangers walked toward us and then approached us. One politely asked, "Do you have a spare cigarette?"

My friends and I didn't smoke because we always strived for strength, beauty, and perfection. So I politely answered, "No, we don't have any—"

I wished I'd been able to finish that sentence before the friend of a friend shouted, "No, we don't have any *&$%*# cigarettes!"

The stranger and his friend were angered by this because they had, in fact, asked nicely. They shouted back, "Whoa! Are we going to have any problems?"

I quickly waved my arms in freak-out motions while saying "No, no, no. No problems. I'm sorry. My friend is a little drunk, so don't listen to him, and I'm sorry we don't have any cigarettes."

The strangers walked away, and we were so grateful that no problems developed.

Until the strangers were around twenty feet away from us and out of nowhere, one of them yelled, "Good thing there weren't going to be any problems because I'd pop a cap in your white boy's a**." Then he reached behind himself and toward his waistline.

My heart dropped.

He pulled out his hand in the shape of gun.

When we were all drunk, something like that was terrifying and might as well have been the real thing.

We all shouted to the effect of, "Whoa, whoa, whoa, man! What the heck! No problems!"

He then put his "gun" back into his imaginary holster.

He walked away again, but he turned around and came back to us, holding his hand behind him, ready to pull out his finger gun again—or possibly a real one.

He then yelled as he approached, "You know what? I've got a problem with you now."

As soon as he was close enough, we were all terrified.

Before he could speak again, I delivered a right hook to his jaw.

He went unconscious and hit the ground with his head so hard it must have cracked the ground.

With him being unconscious, it put all our pride back into our heads, and I immediately went after the other stranger, who had just witnessed his friend getting knocked out right in front of him. Again, we were all in flip flops and tank tops, so I think I remember correctly that one of mine broke during the chasing of the other stranger. I had to stop chasing him and another fantastic friend of mine finished the job.

He tackled the guy and started to punch him repeatedly until he himself was tackled by a complete stranger. Stranger is a bad word for that, let's just stick to the truth of it being a SWAT officer. Why were there a whole bunch of SWAT officers so quickly to get to the scene of this fight?

I'll tell you why, the Freighthouse.

This is a bar and nightclub that is attached to the AAA baseball field, which was an awesome spot to hang out. Especially if there was a baseball game going on. That place recently blew up with crime and fights, even a couple of shootings took place. So, the downtown area had to be flooded with officers.

We all got tackled and handcuffed. I think I remember getting zip ties put on me, which was way worse. I think I still have a scar from it because of how hard the officer put them on. I just remember blood being everywhere on my hands from punching the guy in his teeth. They sat us all down, and by this point there was an ambulance already attending to the stranger.

The guy lay unconscious for what seemed like an hour. By this point the adrenaline and booze was wearing off, and I came to realize that I actually might have badly hurt this guy. Instant regret and fear sunk in, "I might be going to jail. Why did I do that?"

Little did we know, while the paramedics were helping the guy, the officers went into the casino and watched the surveillance tape. Remember when I stated earlier that we were lucky to be right at the halfway point of the block? If we were anywhere further north or south, we would've been out of sight of the cameras.... We had luck.

After getting our side of the story, in which we pleaded and pleaded that we thought he had a gun and even acted like it, we sensed some forgiveness from cops because of three things. First, after what they saw on the tape, it was easy to figure out we weren't lying. Second, they released of all our hands from hand cuffs and zip ties. And lastly, we even got some humor from one of the officers, "You really did that in flip flops?"

We all busted out with laughter. But at this point, we still didn't know if we were going to jail or not.

After another hour, the cops came back, saying we were free to go, saying something that was pretty humorous, "I bet that guy won't do anything like that again. He didn't have a gun, and he can't remember anything, so he can't charge you."

We started to walk back home. By this time the sun had started to come up. We were still shaking but gave each other high fives despite the fact that I was faking the excitement and happy feelings.

I was set free. I didn't like hurting that person, even if

we all felt like he deserved it. Hurting someone to the verge of killing someone is never something to be proud of.

I got lucky, extremely lucky. Or was it luck? Was it time for God to show himself to me?

Nope. Not yet.

And everyone who calls on the name of the Lord will be saved.
(Acts 2:21 NIV)

CHAPTER 13

Therefore, since we have been justified through faith, we have peace with God through our Lord Jesus Christ
(Romans 5:1 NIV)

GUILTY

Tragedy struck my hometown, especially in the sports world. One of the nicest guys in town was hit and killed by a car on a football game weekend. He was the biggest sports news anchor for one of our most popular news stations. Everyone knew him, and everyone adored him. He was especially important to me.

Back in high school, he was the one who broadcasted the top plays of the night for area high schools. My brother and I were often on the news for our awesome games during football. So, I knew this sportscaster's voice, and I knew who he was.

I also knew how devastating it was as a community to experience his passing. I didn't know him personally, but I got a chance to get to know his family. He left behind an amazing wife and three sons. Obviously devastated, they needed help anywhere they could get it.

My cheerleading coach was one of my biggest mentors in my college life. Knowing I was an athletic guy and good with children, my coach asked me if I'd like to hang out with the late sportscaster's kids and play sports with them.

I agreed, especially after hearing about the tragedy. Their dad had been very active in their lives, and playing sports every day after school was routine for them.

The dad was a jack-of-all-trades kind of guy and must have been filled with joy when his kids would ask him to go outside to play catch. In a way, I was replacing him for their after-school stuff. I'd go over there a couple of times a week to hang out with them and make sure they were continuing their sports, just like always.

Then—boom—the mom was diagnosed with breast cancer, as if this family hadn't suffered enough devastation. What the heck? Those poor kids were going through a whirlwind of emotions. They just lost their dad in a freak car accident, and now they're going to lose their mom to breast cancer?

Her cancer ended up being terminal, and she asked to be at home with the kids for the rest of her very low-numbered days. The least I could do was to go and hang out with these soon-to-be-orphaned kids. Luckily, the mom had a sister who was going to take the kids after she passed.

I loved every second of hanging out with those kids. From sports to video games and helping out with homework, I felt like the nicest guy ever. I felt like someone who was helping a family out that *desperately* needed help.

Wait a minute. I wasn't really helping at all. I'd been offered money to hang out with those kids. My heart wasn't fully in it. I didn't *really* care about those kids or their family. It's not like I was a horrible person, but man, does regret start to overfill my soul thinking about my mindset going into it. I didn't know the two greatest commandments back then:

Jesus replied: "'Love the Lord your God with all your heart and with all your soul and with all your mind.' This is the first and greatest commandment. And the second is like it: 'Love your neighbor as yourself.' All the Law and the Prophets hang on these two commandments." (Mathew 22:37-40 NIV)

I specifically remember driving over there sometimes and dreading having to do it. I didn't want to do it anymore. I wasn't a Christian back then; I was selfish. Don't get me wrong: I was a decent human being, and I honestly loved the opportunity to help those kids.

But man, I did it just to "look" like a good human being. I didn't want to fully do it. I just wanted the Brownie points attached to it. My life wasn't fully surrendered to Christ; my heart was still stone.

Eventually, I faded out of their lives. Like a coward, I stopped showing up. I didn't say anything, nor did I text or call about my absence. I didn't think much of it . . . until she passed away.

I didn't even say goodbye. I didn't once pray with her or for her. Today, I would grasp her hands, kneel beside her bed, and pray for her to be healed every dang day. Instead, I didn't do anything, as if that family had gotten in the way of my life. I attended her funeral out of respect, but—man, is this hard and humbling to say—I was almost glad I got my weekday afternoons back.

It's okay to call me a complete jerk. I *was* back then. I've changed now. I understand God's calling on my life. I am to be there for people with empathy and be there for the helpless and broken. I can see why I was like that: I wasn't with Christ. I didn't know what love really meant. I wasn't aware of how my actions could affect those kids.

I feel an overwhelming sense of guilt thinking back on this situation. But, at the same time, I'm glad it happened. Now that God is the ruler of my life, if and when that situation happens again, I will *not* turn my back on others.

I will be there for that family and understand that my

feelings are not the ones that matter. I will be completely obedient to my God's call on my life, which is to love and be there for everyone and anyone.

I wish I'd had a Christian friend back then to knock me upside the head and make me open my eyes. I even remember avoiding my coach who'd given me the opportunity. Oh, and if you haven't picked it up by now—I never hung out with those kids again. What a disgrace. Why did I stop? Why was I jerk?

Because I cared about myself more than I cared about others. Thankfully, that's completely changed. Today I care for others more than myself, tenfold.

You know why? Jesus, that's why.

Praise God for what Ezekiel 36:26–27 says. *"I will give you a new heart and put a new spirit in you; I will remove from you your heart of stone and give you a heart of flesh. And I will put my Spirit in you and move you to follow my decrees and be careful to keep my laws."* (NIV)

Therefore, there is now no condemnation for those who are in Christ Jesus
(Romans 8:1 NIV)

CHAPTER 14

“Watch and pray so that you will not fall into temptation. The spirit is willing, but the flesh is weak” (Matthew 26:41 NIV).

DEAR DAD

Dad, first off, I love you. Most importantly, I forgive you. I really do. You didn't know.

Athleticism was only the beginning of your teaching. Succeeding in every single sport was a staple of my identity. Thank you for teaching me how to hunt, how to fish, and even how to grip the axe correctly to chop decent wood for the fireplace. You know—all the testosterone-building stuff you need in life, the things you need to be able to do to support the family. What kind of household would you have if you're unable to fix things, be the person to rely on, the provider? There's always something to be said about working hard and being humble while you do it. It's a great feeling knowing that if anything "manly" comes up, I'll be able to handle it. So, thank you.

Most kids grow up in the sports world without their parents attending one game. I can tell you with one-hundred percent confidence that you showed up to every single one. From basketball, baseball, and football games, you were the man of all men when it came to sports. You taught me how to swing a golf club, how to shoot a basketball, and how to catch and throw a football. Some kids need a coach to motivate them and be an ultimate dad replacement. But

I didn't need that—I had you for the sports world. I had you for the character-building world. You taught me what hard work is, what's necessary to be good at a sport, and how to be successful in the sports world.

I remember staying at my aunt's house when my twin brother and I had to be left there for the night. Mom had to go to work for the graveyard shift at the post office. With no one at home while she worked, we had to go somewhere else—somewhere we didn't belong. It wasn't home. We slept on a simple pull-out couch in the living room. I didn't have any understanding of the situation then, but now I know.

I wish you could see how much God loves you. I not only think that you need him, but he desperately wants you. He wants your attention, and I believe that you can help a lot of people. I think that you can use your voice on a bigger platform, that you can say that you've surrendered. What you've been through and done can help so many people—we are all sinners; temptation is a daily battle.

I'm not saying this out of hate; I just wish you'd listen to me. I just wish you could understand how many people you could help through the stigmas of temptation.

Be a brave dad. You've made mistakes. You've been there, and you can help people through it all, and you can understand what it takes to be a married man and what not to do now. It hasn't led to anything other than unhappiness for you.

I don't know what makes you happy. Reach out to God. If you surrender your life to him and understand that he loves you, he's going to show you what real love is.

I forgive you. I just don't know how to talk to you about this. I love you so dang much. Allowing my judgment on sin to be controlled by the love of God makes forgiveness easy.

My Heavenly Father did do one great thing to my heart: He made me look forward to having a family and a wife and doing things right. If only you really knew God, and if only you knew how much I love you—your life could be much greater, if you'd follow him and his advice for you.

Love your son,

Zack

❧

"Each of you should use whatever gift you have received to serve others, as faithful stewards of God's grace in its various forms. If anyone speaks, they should do so as one who speaks the very words of God. If anyone serves, they should do so with the strength God provides, so that in all things God may be praised through Jesus Christ. To him be the glory and the power forever and ever. Amen." (1 Peter 4:10–11 NIV)

This chapter was the hardest to write: being brave wasn't enough to put these words on this paper. It was just getting it over with and understanding that it was such a huge part of who I was. Let me be straight: this was not a blast-my-dad chapter. This is how I feel.

God helped me understand that forgiveness is important. I'm transparent enough to say that I had "Daddy Issues," and that's the truth. So, I wrote a letter. Simple as that.

For those of you who think you had the worst dad, if you had an absent dad, my hope is for you is to understand that not every dad is perfect. I mean, let's get real here: no dad is perfect. They're all sinners and were born into sin, and we're always going to be sinners.

Now, do you think I can say that my dad could've done a little bit better with his self-control? Sure, but that doesn't mean I don't love him, or that I don't forgive him. You may have yet to forgive your father. You may have yet to forgive him for his mistakes, and they probably eat at you and your soul more than they affect him.

Work on forgiving him. Let that weight off your shoulders. Understand that once it's over, he can't take it back. You need to forgive him, not only for certain things, but completely forgive him for *everything*. I promise your relationship will get better.

Abandonment is the only word that comes to my mind when it comes to my father. Why? Because he was abandoned just like my brother and me. One thing I needed to understand is that he simply didn't know what he was doing. He didn't understand what love was; he hadn't learned it from anybody. His parents got divorced as well, so what did I think was going to happen? He didn't know how to treat his family or how to treat his spouse. The only thing he'd seen from his parents was divorce. What he had experienced as a kid was exactly what I'd experienced: divorce.

As a kid, having your parents get separated develops scars only God can fix.

So, my dad is not to blame. He had the same unfortunate upbringing that we did. He learned how to play sports and how to be a man but never learned the real definition of love, how to love your family, or how to love your wife.

If only he would listen, he could learn that from God. Love is from God; God is the definition of love, so if anybody knows what he's talking about, it's God. How can you know how to love if you haven't developed a relationship with the one who *is* love?

It's hard putting your own feelings behind the feelings of your family or your wife. It's incredibly hard, especially when you don't have God in your life telling you what to do. So it's difficult listening to your father or listening to anybody else when no one has been completely there for you.

What if I told you that someone *is* there for you? Each and every step of your life has guidance, a Father directing and commanding you on what to do—in your family, in your relationships, in your everyday life situations. You have hope.

My dad had no one he was listening to, and I forgive him for that.

Get rid of all bitterness, rage and anger, brawling and slander, along with every form of malice. Be kind and compassionate to one another, forgiving each other, just as in Christ God forgave you.

(Ephesians 4:31-32 NIV)

CONCLUSION

"I have told you these things, so that in me you may have peace. In this world you will have trouble. But take heart! I have overcome the world."
(John 16:33 NIV)

11/15/2015 is the date of my baptism.

11/08/2015 is the day I surrendered my life to Christ.

The point of this book is to NEVER forget where I came from. All the tears, all the heartbreaks, all the times I was in the shower, on the floor, sobbing, not wanting to move. Asking myself, *What are you even doing here.... what's the point?*

The pain was so real, so devastating. I don't ever want to make those mistakes again. I never want to live that life without the gospel of Jesus Christ. I have so much freedom within God's grace that it would be IMPOSSIBLE to go back. The freedom has allowed me to be open about all the horrible things that I've done. I know there's worse out there, but this was *my* worst, and it hurt pretty dang bad.

I'm glad it happened. I'll take God and the Gospel over anything I've ever had or will have in this life.

I'm not sure if I wanted to end this book with a *what you should do* ending...but I decided to just give you a few ideas...Hoping this gives you inspiration to live a life for Christ, and if you are already living for Christ, keep going. Also, Christ follower or not, I just want to let you know from the bottom of my heart, reach out to me. If you ever want to get something off your chest or open up about anything. I'm here for you. I mean it. Now on to a couple things you should try.

- Sit down and write down your testimony. This could take some time, but if it's the most important thing in your life, which it should be, it's worth it. This book was my way of writing my testimony down. So sit down, put some worship music on and start writing. Doesn't have to be long. Frame it and never forget it.
- Be Brave about your problems and share them with people who TRULY care about you and, most importantly, share them with God.
- Create an "I exist" statement, two to three sentences of why YOU are on this planet. Take this to heart. Figure out your gifts, your talents and really think hard. This is mine: "I exist to humbly use my gift of connectivity to inspire and motivate by leading by example. Never ceasing to grow God's kingdom. With grace first, I surrender everything."
- Think about giving your life to Christ. The forgiveness you receive for everything you've

> done is relentless. If nothing else, just try to find out where you're going when you die. Really think about it. This is your soul I'm talking about.

Quickly turn to the back cover again. See that? See the smile that I have? That smile is the result of Jesus Christ helping me overcome all these issues.

Jesus is reaching out his hand.

Will you give him yours?

Be Brave.

YOUR FREE EBOOK

Join the CKN Christian Publishing mailing list for information on new releases, updates, discount offers and your FREE copy of Why Does a Mockingbird Sing?

http://christiankindlenews.com/get-free-copy-mockingbird-sing/

Thank you for taking the time to read Be Brave. If you enjoyed it, please consider telling your friends or posting a short review. Word of mouth is an author's best friend and much appreciated.

Thank you.
Zack Quilici

ABOUT THE AUTHOR

Author Zack Quilici wants to be known as someone that lives his life for Christ and nothing else. Pursuing a Pastoral career, he resides in the beautiful San Diego region of Vista, California. He attends Northcoast Church and is a small part of the Junior High youth program.

Growing up in Reno, Nevada he is no stranger to activity. From football, basketball, snowboarding, golf, volleyball and Crossfit, you name the sport, he's there. He's been coaching fitness for almost 8 years and just loves when people get their first pull up!

For more information:

christiankindlenews.com/our-authors/zack-quilici/
facebook.com/ZQbeBRAVE
instagram: @zack_quilici